NCEA PAPERS

TEAM TEACHING: A RATIONALE

by Melvin P. Heller, D.Ed.

National Catholic Educational Association
NCEA Papers, Box 667, Dayton, Ohio 45401

ABOUT THE AUTHOR

Dr. Melvin P. Heller is an Associate Professor in the Department of Education at Loyola University, Chicago. In an outstanding career as an educator he has been Assistant Director, Administrative Research Department, Educational Research Council of Greater Cleveland; Assistant Superintendent—Curriculum Director, Ridgewood High School, District 234, Norridge, Ill.; and Superintendent of School District 61, Clarendon Hills, Ill.; and has taught on all levels, from the elementary school to the university. He holds B.A. and M.A. degrees from De Paul University in Chicago and a doctorate in education from Loyola. Dr. Heller has written and lectured widely. He is married and has four children.

BACKGROUND

Teamwork, teamwork, teamwork. We have examples of this cooperation in so many fields that the idea is hardly an innovation. From medicine to athletics, the planning and its implementation require the sharing, the give-and-take of many talents and insights. The example of "teaming" is all around us, even in schools. Good schools have always operated as a team: administrators, teachers, specialists, consultants, and so forth. Looked at in this light, team teaching is not to be feared as a totally new concept which will threaten teachers. On the contrary, team teaching can help the teachers gain competence and confidence. As the explosion of knowledge increases and the intellectual demands on a single teacher increase, the ability of this teacher to keep apace of his field decreases. The promise afforded by regular, purposeful, professional cooperation is too significant in the field of education to be ignored.

Although the origins of team teaching are not new, the formal label is approximately ten years old. Thus, team teaching qualifies as an innovation. On the high school level, Dr. J. Lloyd Trump, of the National Association of Secondary-School Principals, provided the leadership to popularize the team approach. On the elementary school level, leadership was provided by the SUPRAD project at Harvard University. During the ten or so years of its life the concept of team teaching has received much publicity. It has been tried in one form or another in schools in every part of the United States as well as in some schools in foreign countries.

What is team teaching all about? It is about articulation of content, appropriateness of method, cooperation among teachers, and individualization of staff and student roles.

This Paper is devoted to an exploration of some of the main features of team teaching. The treatment is intended to be a blend of the theoretical and the practical. The advantages of team teaching will be stressed because the writer cannot subdue his enthusiasm for the efficacy of the team approach to teaching and to learning.

DEFINITION AND PURPOSES

Team teaching is a cooperative effort of two or more teachers with complementary academic strengths who work on a *regular* and purposeful basis to plan, to prepare, to present, and to evaluate learning experiences. As such, team teaching is more than a mere method. It is a means to achieve certain ends: to improve curriculum, to professionalize teaching and to individualize instruction. The team approach allows teachers and students to develop special strengths and to share these strengths with peers. Usually, some type of schedule modification is necessary so that the greatest benefits can be derived.

Additional comments concerning the major purposes are in order:

1. *Improvement of curriculum.*—The team of teachers can focus attention on curriculum concerns so that new and old content can be taught with meaning and viability.

2. *Professionalization of teaching.*—The team which is organized on the

6   basis of complementary teacher talents can emphasize its strengths and minimize its weaknesses. Moreover, the team can provide valuable in-service advantages to all members. With a flexible schedule the teachers will have time to think and to confer with each other on school time. If funds are available, teacher aides can help to provide time for professional people to perform professional tasks.

3. *Individualization of instruction.*—When the students are permitted to learn in the formalized structure of large groups, the more permissive structure of small-group discussions, and the relative freedom of independent study, they can grow into self-reliant, self-directed learners. The degree of freedom should be commensurate with the ability and maturity of the students to accept this freedom. In general, as the students go from freshmen to seniors, their freedom should be greater and greater. The following diagram illustrates this point:

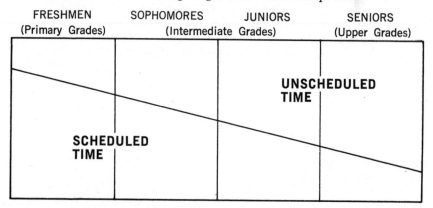

FRESHMEN	SOPHOMORES	JUNIORS	SENIORS
(Primary Grades)	(Intermediate Grades)		(Upper Grades)

ESSENTIAL FEATURES

The attraction of team teaching, as is true of every bona fide innovation, is that it lends itself to many modifications which, in effect, become innovations themselves. There are so many cooperative endeavors in schools that new labels are now being sought to identify the efforts. The popularity of the many variations on the team teaching theme is testimony to the flexibility of the approach. Yet some basic ingredients must be acknowledged so that a common framework can be established in this treatment of the subject. Regardless of what else is involved, team teaching *must* incorporate several essential features:

1. Two or more teachers.
2. Real teamwork on a regular basis.
3. Large-group, small-group, and individual study aspects of learning.

Admittedly, these essentials leave much room for modification as they are employed in specific settings. The flexibility of the schedules, specific talents of teachers and students, administrative leadership, curriculum emphasis, are but a few of the considerations which will determine team composition, subject and/or grades involved, and allocation of time concerning large-group, small-group, and individual study approaches. Each

school can and must make its own decisions on these and related concerns. 7
Specific and detailed, hard-and-fast rules limit the flexibility which is so
crucial to the team approach. Imagination, creativity, and, above all, intelligence should guide the individual school staff in how it adapts its adop-
tion of teaming.

TYPES OF OBJECTIONS

Among school administrators there are some who accept team teaching in
theory but not in practice. These administrators recognize the many educational challenges and opportunities presented by team teaching, but they
can find many reasons to resist its implementation. Typical of the objections
are these:

1. It costs too much money.
2. The staff is not ready.
3. We have insufficient space and facilities.
4. We don't know how to begin.
5. We are not sure of the outcome.
6. The schedule is too complicated.
7. How do we know that our teachers can work together well?

Reactions of this type are wholesome and should be encouraged. The fact
that serious thought is given to the team approach is a good indication that
acceptance or rejection of the idea will be carefully considered. This
careful consideration necessitates long-range and short-range planning, and
it minimizes the temptation to innovate solely because it is fashionable.

NEED FOR PLANNING

The administrator must be willing to spend time on intelligent and careful
planning *before* the team teaching begins. To do otherwise is to insure
failure. Unfortunately, many schools have tried, and are still trying, to
gain all of the advantages of team teaching by using only certain aspects
of the approach. This is wishful thinking at best and educational travesty
at worst. For example, large-group instruction without small-group discussion
cannot produce the greatest educational dividends.

The careful planning must include the obvious factors of goals, personnel,
content, instructional materials, and facilities. The coordination of these
and other factors requires administrative skill. Even if the undertaking is
on a very limited scale of one level of one subject, details of planning
must be considered. The person in charge need not be the principal, but
the principal's support is essential.

Another point regarding planning is in order. The need for care does
not mean everlasting timidity and hesitancy. One cannot wait forever before
trying something different. This is especially true if one believes that there
is merit in the change. Team teaching has been tried in enough schools
to merit its position as a worthy educational innovation. Whether it is
most appropriate in a given school is a matter for individual decision. It
is certain, however, that with care and cultivation, team teaching can
work excellently in any school.

Another valuable outcome of the planning and the raising of objections is that specific questions can be formulated. A representative list of questions and answers follows: [1]

1. **What are the purposes of team teaching?**
   Team teaching is not a mere method. It is a means to curricular improvement, professionalization of teaching, and the individualization of instruction.

2. **What are some major advantages of team teaching?**
   In addition to the advantages of achieving the main purposes, team teaching provides professional opportunities for the following:
   a) Staff involvement with curriculum concerns.
   b) Abundant opportunities for leadership and followership.
   c) Peer-group recognition.
   d) The nongraded approach.
   e) Individual study opportunities in depth.
   f) Involvement of "special" teachers (librarians, guidance counselors, teachers of art and music) in the "regular" class offerings.
   g) Teacher planning time during the school day through schedule modifications.
   h) In-service education advantages.
   i) Opportunities for teacher specialization as well as expansion of areas of broad knowledge in related fields.
   j) Expansion of supervisory roles of peers and administrators.
   k) Opportunities for teachers and students to have variety during the school day.

3. **What are some disadvantages?**
   The major disadvantages deal with attitudes of team members:
   a) Failure to communicate clearly, freely, and openly.
   b) Lack of attention paid to details and follow-up activities.
   c) Possibility that teachers may idle away time.
   d) Possibility that teachers may not evaluate each other on a professional basis.
   e) Possibility that a prima donna may emerge.
   None of these problems is insurmountable. Real teamwork can solve these difficulties.

4. **How can a school begin team teaching?**
   Start with the teachers who are most eager and able to cooperate and who are aware of the significance and purposes of team teaching. Details on implementation are stated elsewhere in this Paper.

5. **How do departmentalization and team teaching differ?**
   In departmentalization teachers "divvy up" the teaching load; in team teaching they share the total load. Unlike departmentalization, where teaching assignments are separated into neat but artificial niches, where teachers need not communicate often, and where

[1] For a more extensive treatment of questions and answers see Heller, M. P., *Team Teaching*, Cleveland: Educational Research Council of Greater Cleveland, 1963.

correlation may be absent, team teaching is a bulwark against the compartmentalization of knowledge. In team teaching the teachers work together on the lessons and activities for their course, whether the course is on one or more grade and subject levels. Although teacher specialization is encouraged in teaming, each team member is involved to some degree in all phases of the team effort. Thus, in departmentalization the course is *mine;* in team teaching the course is *ours.*

6. **What is a flexible schedule?**

Details are given in another section of this Paper. In general, however, the schedule must provide opportunities during the school day for a variety of teaching-learning activities, including large-group instruction, small-group discussion, and individual study. Variations in the schedule in the length of periods (modules) and from day to day are common. The schedule can range from limited to great flexibility depending upon the degree of team involvement and the provisions for the three essential phases of the program.

7. **What is the recommended time allotment for each phase of team teaching?**

There is no pat answer to this question, but the most frequently cited percentages are 40 percent for large group, 30 percent for small group, and 30 percent for individual study. As the student progresses, these figures should be altered to provide more time for individual study.

8. **Can ability groups be used?**

Ability groups can certainly be used. In the large group there may be broad divisions in terms of upper half and lower half according to student ability. In the small group, students who are scheduled at the same time slot can be moved easily from sub-group to sub-group according to interest, ability, introversion, extroversion, and so forth.

9. **Which subjects are best adapted to team teaching?**

All subjects on all levels can be adapted effectively if the team approaches the task at hand with interest, intelligence, and professionalism. Large-group (the telling and demonstrating phase), small-group (the discussion phase), and individual study aspects of each subject can be determined by the team of teachers. They can stay within the boundaries of a given subject, they may cross subject matter lines, or they may cross subject *and* grade level lines. The decision is theirs.

10. **What is the importance of visuals?**

Visuals serve many important purposes, especially in large-group instruction. They help to crystallize abstractions for students; they enliven the presentation; they serve to highlight what the teacher considers to be important; they guide the teacher in his comments; and they serve as a record of what was presented. Moreover, they present a challenge to the team of teachers who must find ways to translate verbalizations into meaningful visual representations.

11. Which aspect of team teaching is most difficult for teachers?
Most teachers have problems with small-group discussions because they seldom have the knowledge and experience to employ effective group dynamics techniques. Usually these teachers abuse the small-group setting by lecturing and/or by dominating the students. With practice, however, teachers and students learn that a small group is for the purpose of student-centered discussions.

12. Which aspect is most difficult for students?
Although students generally enjoy the small-group discussion opportunities, they sometimes have difficulties in adjusting to the situation. Usually the difficulties diminish as experience and ability develop.

Difficulties with independent study are more serious, but they are not as easily recognized. It is easy to keep students busy with routine work during unscheduled time, and many need this structure, but the true goal of self-directiveness is elusive. Provocative, open-ended assignments by teachers may lead to self-selected, self-directed learning of students.

13. How can teachers evaluate pupil progress?
Evaluation becomes a team effort. Two or more teachers become involved in the determination of a student's grade. With knowledge of large-group, small-group, and individual study aspects of the learning situation, many factors and several viewpoints can be incorporated into this grade determination. The conferences for this purpose may lead the team to acknowledge that there are many intangible aspects of learning which, although subjectively evaluated, are important and which cannot be assessed by paper-and-pencil tests. Thus, hopefully, the concept of pupil evaluation will be broadened.

14. How are the student-teacher relationships affected?
The relationships can become closer in small-group and in individual study settings than is usually possible in a conventional classroom. In these settings the teachers can observe and work with students on a very informal basis. The nature of large-group instruction does not require close student-teacher contact, although the good relationships developed may enhance the learning in this phase.

15. What is the importance of learning centers?
It is in the learning centers (sometimes called resource centers) where most of the individual study leading to independent study takes place. Ideally, these centers are separate rooms located in various parts of the school, but they can be a part of existing classrooms and libraries, renovated storage areas, hallways, basements, and offices. Each center should be equipped with books, charts, periodicals, tapes, and other materials of instruction. If possible there should be a learning center for each major subject area or broad field area. Teachers of these subjects should be available often to work with students. The schedule can provide the time for this help. By coordinating the activities of the learning centers with the library resources, the library can be the hub of the school.

16. How can the administrator insure teacher cooperation?
The administrator has no guarantee on this matter, but teachers will cooperate without force if they see the need. Hence, the administrator's task is to help to develop, nurture, and guide the concept of cooperation. This teamwork is important not only for the team teachers but also for other staff members. For example, individual and independent study cannot thrive unless teachers work together. A teacher may be willing to send a student to a study area, but another teacher may not be willing to receive the student. During unscheduled time a student can be thwarted if facilities, materials, and/or teacher assistance are not available. Independent study is self-directed, but real teamwork with administrative leadership will facilitate this direction.

17. What financial considerations are necessary?
If team teaching is undertaken on a limited basis (two-six teachers for two-three subjects), the expenses need not be much more than those in a conventional setting. Perhaps the only increase in the budget would be due to additional audiovisual equipment and supplies.

If the program expands throughout the building, the expenditures can increase. However, careful planning of the budget can result in different allocations of finance rather than more spending. For instance, the total number of teachers needed in team teaching may be equal to the requisite number in a conventional setting. The trick is to reassign the staff instead of adding more members. In team teaching, teacher time, physical space, and materials of instruction are used differently and so financial savings in one area may cover the increased cost in another. Chalk boards, for instance, may not be needed in large-group instruction rooms. The money saved can go to purchase something else.

ELABORATIONS ON SOME OF THESE CONCERNS

The brevity of the foregoing answers will not be adequate for those who are deeply interested in this topic. Therefore, certain concerns and issues related to team teaching have been isolated for lengthier development.

Teacher Factors
As the team progresses, teacher talents for one or more of the phases may become apparent. Until the specific competencies of the team teachers are known, it may be wise to involve all team members in all phases of instruction.

If the staff resources are to be used most effectively, then team members and the administration will allow the competencies of the teachers to be made available to the students. Teacher talent is a valuable resource, and it should be extended widely. Therefore, the skillful lecturer can, and should, lecture frequently. Each team must decide whether it wishes to develop the "jack-of-all-trades"; the expert lecturer, the expert seminar leader, and the expert individual study teacher; or a combination of these extremes. The team may prefer to involve all members in all of these phases. This is a decision for the individual team to make. Again, the

need for close cooperation is clear, but administrators should not make final decisions too soon.

The talents of the teachers and the administrators bring up the matter of qualifications of team members.[2] Age, years of experience, degrees, subject area seem to make no difference regarding team teaching performance. Teacher qualities of intelligence, curiosity, creativity, ability, enthusiasm, and leadership, as they apply to willingness to change, are of great and obvious importance. Regardless of what other qualifications the teachers may have, the crucial ingredients are cooperation and pliability. Without these, there can be no team effort. The teacher must be able to work well with peers and students without damage to his own ego. He must be able to cooperate, to suggest, and to compromise without sacrificing his own basic principles. He must be able to see the other person's point of view and be pliable enough and secure enough to experiment with it. If all of the team members are pliable, not in the sense of being weak or easily influenced but in the sense of being intelligently flexible, they will be quick to realize the success or failure of the experimentation, and they can make the necessary modifications.

Teachers and administrators who work together, who will welcome constructive criticism, and who will discuss curriculum ideas freely cannot fail to improve their course offerings. In working closely with curriculum development, capable team teachers will be able to formulate large-group, small-group, and individualized approaches to their academic offerings so that these can be made most meaningful for the students. Team teaching encourages creative, imaginative, capable teachers and administrators to experiment with what they consider to be improvements upon the status quo. There is no fear of chaos if intelligence guides these innovations.

A note of warning must be sounded at this point. Seldom, if ever, is an entire staff ready to embark upon an innovation. Not all teachers can be, nor want to be, team teachers. They are successful in their own right, and they are not convinced that a change is best for them. Perhaps they are correct, and their wishes should be respected. If team teaching stresses individualization, it is ridiculous to contradict this emphasis by trying to force every teacher and student into its mold. Rather than try to involve everyone, it is prudent to begin with those staff members who are interested in the innovations. To wait for everyone is as unrealistic as it is frustrating for those who wish to step forward.

The team teachers can do much to share the load equitably in terms of academic, professional, and personal strengths, and to discourage lackadaisical behavior by any member of the teaching team. The administration must also exert the kind of influence and pressure which will permit teachers to be free to think and to teach creatively *and* to respect their colleagues and their students.

These comments bring up the topic of leadership in team teaching.

Leadership in Team Teaching

It is imperative that team teachers possess qualities which will enable them to lead and to follow. This is true because there are opportunities for

[2] For a broader treatment of this topic see Chapter 10, "Qualities for Team Members," *Team Teaching, Bold New Venture* (Beggs, ed.), Indiana University Press, 1965.

14 rotating leadership on every team. A definition of leadership may help to clarify these ideas. The following working definition can be offered as a guide: *Leadership exists when a person called leader inspires others called followers to work cooperatively to achieve goals which they agree to be desirable.* The democratic overtones of the preceding are evident. The implications of hierarchy are also evident. Although team teaching encourages individuality among teachers, the success of a team teaching effort is dependent to a great degree upon how well the team performs within the school hierarchy. Although necessary, this hierarchy must not be a barrier to emergent leadership.

In another publication, the author and a colleague have written the following comments on the subject of hierarchy and team teaching:

> Despite the assumed equality within a "team" of teachers, it seems that, inevitably, a natural hierarchy will emerge. Regardless of the number of worthwhile ideas offered by members of a team, these ideas need purpose and direction. One, or perhaps two, members of the group will take the initiative to consolidate these ideas into workable form. These two will probably be conceded the leadership of the group because of the inability or the lack of desire on the part of the others to assume responsibility for the progress of the group. Whether or not these people are designated by the administration in advance, there *will* be one or two who, necessarily, will become the acknowledged leaders and organizers of the team.

> The question of natural leadership is of the utmost importance. There is some leadership in every group and, of course, this generalization includes every faculty. The persons who are leaders have status, whether or not this status is officially designated by the administration. Certainly, the best situation exists when the person who has been given the title of leader, and is therefore the leader by virtue of authority, is also the person who is accepted by the group as the natural leader. The administration and the designated team leaders must be alert to the signs of conflict which result inevitably when there is a significant breach between leadership by titular position and leadership which emerges from the peer group.

> In some cases, if there is a difference between the natural leadership and the designated team leadership, no conflict may result. The designated team leaders may willingly (or perhaps unwittingly) relinquish much of their authority to a natural leader among the group. Perhaps these "leaders" who do not possess the strength attributed to them by the administration may be forced by the team itself to concede decisions to others who show an aptitude and capacity for being decisive and definite in their appraisal and conclusion.[3]

Not only is leadership necessary on a given team, but also it is necessary on the part of the school officials. As stated before, the leadership on a given team need not be designated. The leadership opportunities and responsibilities will vary in accordance with the type of subject matter

[3] "Hierarchy in Team Teaching," *NASSP Bulletin*, December, 1962, pp. 59-64 (Co-author, Elizabeth Belford).

offering at any given time. In those instances where the involvement in
team teaching is great, it is wise to have permanent, designated leaders.
These leaders may be a team leader, a team chairman, a department head,
a principal, or a supervisor. The determination of leadership is a matter for
each individual school to decide. The importance of leadership responsibilities, however, exists in all situations. The communication complexities
involved in a team situation require that someone be responsible for the
coordination of these communications. Responsibility without authority is
precarious. Responsibility with authority is effective when the leader does
not abuse his authority.

In view of these considerations, pertinent comments must be made about
the leadership role of the designated leaders. For those schools which involve
themselves in team teaching situations on a small scale, the comments will
be appropriate as a guide to future implementation. For those schools
which are involved in team teaching on a large scale, the comments may
be appropriate for present implementation.

The Principal.—The administrator in a school where team teaching
exists can serve a leadership role in a variety of ways. Perhaps the most
important way is to exert a positive influence toward the team activities by
providing moral support to the teachers. In order to provide this support,
the administrator must believe that team teaching is a valuable and efficient
means to achieve the end of improvement of the teaching-learning situation.
The principal must be willing to effect the attitudinal changes necessary to
make this viewpoint his conviction. If the administrator is unable to see
the advantages of team teaching for his staff and for their students, the
lack of administrative approbation may cause the team effort to founder
and fail.

It is true that the administrator will have ample opportunities to develop
leadership skills through experience in a team teaching program. For the
purpose of this discussion, however, the following assumptions are made:

1. The administrator has leadership ability.
2. The administrator understands the subtleties as well as the obvious
   considerations attendant to team teaching endeavors.
3. The administrator accepts team teaching as worthy of his time and
   effort.

The involvement of a staff in a team teaching situation forces the administrator to focus some of his attention upon the instructional program.
This attention is necessary for any administrator who wishes to keep pace
with the progress of team teaching. Team teaching can provide for the
administrator an opportunity to be the instructional leader of his school.
The principal may have subject matter strengths which are unknown to his
teachers. For example, he may be the outstanding expert in the school on
modern mathematics. If he attends planning sessions, he will be able to
contribute significantly to the development of learning experiences. Some
teachers may be surprised to find that the principal is more than a mere
clerk. The principal may be surprised to learn that he is a valuable member

16 of the instructional team. In fact, he will be able to participate actively as a team member in the classroom. When the academic strength of the principal is necessary for the success of the teaching situation, he can lecture and/or involve himself in small-group discussion classes. In most schools, the principal's work load does not allow frequent teaching assignments, but the principal who is interested in team teaching can find the time, on occasion, to engage in instruction. A competent clerk is of inestimable value in freeing the principal to provide instructional leadership. No school can afford the luxury of *not* having a good clerk who can take over many of the routine duties of principals. The value of the principal's classroom activities can be justified in many ways, including increased insights into team teaching and the advantage of demonstration teaching.

In addition to planning and teaching opportunities, the supervisory function of the principal becomes quite important. The objectives of his supervisory visits must be clearly understood by all. As is true in all types of school organizations, a follow-up conference to discuss the visitation is necessary. If these visits and conferences are to be effective and clearly understood, the administrator and the teachers must consider themselves part of the same team, a team which is dedicated to the improvement of instruction.

The leadership role of the administrator as it relates to effective team teaching can be treated broadly in two categories. The administrator must provide the *physical structure* and *psychological structure* if the team approach is to be successful.

Physical Structure.—The kinds of considerations necessary for the physical structure of a team organization can tax the ingenuity of the administrator. These considerations, however, do not present insurmountable problems. The physical setting must be appropriate for team teaching. This physical setting includes the space, the equipment, the facilities, and the supplies necessary. New buildings can be designed to fit the team approach. In new buildings, the design can provide the flexibility of space and facilities as they relate to team teaching. Room sizes should vary to allow large-group and small-group classes to meet in an environment which is conducive to learning. Individual study areas should be designed to permit serious, private study to take place. In old buildings, the room problem is often solved by the removal and/or the addition of walls and partitions, by replacing the permanently affixed desks, and by modifying the uses of existing rooms. The salient point is that the physical facilities necessary to implement team teaching can be made available through practical allocation of space.

A major difficulty for the administrator is the development of a schedule which will make possible the best utilization of the physical setting and which is flexible enough to provide the kinds of instruction necessary for effective team teaching. This topic will be treated with more detail in another section of this Paper. For the purpose of this discussion, it is sufficient to say that the schedule can be tailor-made for team teaching purposes. Every interested principal can solve the problems related to the physical structure of a team teaching organization.

Psychological Structure.—The administrative provisions for the psychological structure of a team teaching situation are very challenging. It is readily
understood that team teaching involves an attitudinal change on the part of
the teachers on the team. As stated before, this change in attitude is required
of the administrator, also. With intelligent administrative guidelines, the
changes necessary need not be traumatic for those involved. The principal
should make certain that all involved understand why the change from the
conventional school organization to team teaching is made.

Once understood by all, great changes are possible. It is important to
underscore the following as an administrative guide. *The behavior change
of teachers is **not** slow and their security is **not** threatened when the instructional environment, although new, is consistent and logical.* The newness
of the team teaching situation helps the individuals to try adaptations, and
the consistency gives direction and makes the adaptations more comfortable.
There is much in team teaching which is very similar to elements in a
conventional school. If the required change for the teachers is structured
so that there is enough of the old to give them a feeling of familiarity,
the innovations can be made with a minimum of difficulty.

If the teachers do not understand the changes in their professional role,
many problems may develop. The time that the administrator spends to
help the team teachers to understand their roles in large-group, small-group,
and individual study situations is time well spent. For example, a teacher
who does not understand his role in a student-centered discussion or in
an individual study situation may believe erroneously that his presence
is unnecessary in these phases of instruction. A teacher may not realize
that although pupils can learn much by themselves, the guidance of this
learning is a professional obligation. Teachers have been known to leave
small groups and/or individuals unattended regularly for long periods of
time. The reasons given reflect more of an interest in cigarettes and coffee
than in students. Although such gross ignorance and/or indifference is
the exception rather than the rule, it is significant enough if practiced
at all to warrant disgust and immediate rejection. If the errant teacher
merely misunderstood his role in small-group and individual study activities,
the administration and the team members should help the teacher to
develop an insight and deeper knowledge about his role. If the errant
teacher tried to take selfish advantage of the pupil-centered activities, he
should not be allowed to develop this inclination. Whether the means of
clarification are democratic or autocratic, the errant behavior must cease.

The Team Leader.—All that has been said about the leadership role
of the principal applies, through delegation, to the team leader. In those
schools where team teaching is on so broad a scale that this designation is
necessary, the role of the team leader is very important. His subject
matter strengths and his leadership qualities will be put to many tests.
The team leader's role may be divided into three aspects: administrator,
supervisor, teacher.

Administrator.—The administrative demands require attention to details,
scheduling, planning meetings, coordinating the use of large-group, small-
group, and individual study facilities, spot assignments of teachers, and

coordination of the work of teacher aides. The principal of the building is ultimately responsible for all of the preceding duties, but the delegation of these to a team leader may improve team efficiency. The team leader is generally in much closer contact with team members than is the principal.

Supervisor.—The supervisory duties of team leaders include the supervision of classes, follow-up conferences, offerings of suggestions for improvement, making recommendations and formulating evaluations of team members and team progress, helping the teachers to evaluate pupil progress, coordinating lesson plans, and assisting in the determination of professional value judgments. The effective team leader with the above responsibilities should have the authority to make final decisions when the team members reach an impasse. Moreover, in the interest of improved instruction, the team leader should help to determine what to include and what to exclude in terms of content considerations. These determinations will be a challenge to the academic strengths and the leadership skills of the team leader.

Teacher.—The administrative and supervisory duties of team leaders may lessen their teaching load. It is wise, however, for team leaders to remain a part of the teaching team. Their teaching performances not only will keep them in close contact with students and content, but also will serve as good examples of good teaching. The teaching duties of team leaders may include large-group instruction, small-group instruction, individual study activities, use of audiovisual aids, and demonstration lessons.

The team leader has an obligation to keep alert professionally. When successful, he will be able to inspire his team members to increase their professional awareness. The more stable, the more professional, the more knowledgeable the team leader, the more effective he will be as an inspiration to his fellow team members.

As stated above, the designated team leader may be a principal, a supervisor, a department head, or some other competent staff member. The role of this person with team members is essentially the same as his role with all teachers. The main difference is the closer contact with team members than with the faculty in general. If the team teachers are to be receptive to change, then the team leader must be even more receptive. This great degree of receptivity to change, however, must be guided with caution. The role of influence of the team leader forces a kind of restraint upon him so that he will not inspire his followers to run off in all directions. In this light, there is no contradiction between stability and wise change.

In the spring of 1961, the author, who was then the assistant superintendent and curriculum director at the Ridgewood High School District in Norridge, Illinois, developed an opinionnaire which attempted to evaluate some of the qualities of leadership desirable in a team leader. (See page 39 for the complete opinionnaire.) The six qualities were these:

1. Ability to implement the basic objectives of the program.
2. Ability to create an atmosphere in which a teacher can work well.
3. Ability to give clear and reasonable directions.
4. Interest in providing opportunities for the teacher to engage in planning.
5. Availability for personal conferences.
6. Willingness to work long hours on school problems.

The teachers, all of whom were involved in team teaching regardless of the subject matter, evaluated the team leaders on a five-point continuum, ranging from superior to poor. In every leadership quality listed, the team leaders were rated from average to superior by the staff. Although these qualities in themselves have implications of leadership, they represent little more than an initial attempt to evaluate leadership. Moreover, the evaluations thus far have been subjective. The list and the evaluations are valuable, however, if they serve as nothing more than a point of departure for other schools which attempt to isolate and to evaluate some leadership qualities.

Leadership opportunities exist in abundance in a team teaching situation. Leadership qualities can be learned. Once learned, they can be developed expertly. In harmony with the concept of learn-by-doing, the emergence of leaders in a team situation will be a direct outgrowth of the involvement of the team in a variety of activities. As stated before, in a complex team teaching organization, the designation of leaders is essential to maximum efficiency. These designated leaders must have the responsibility, the authority, and the ability to lead. In those situations where no one is designated as the leader, natural leaders will emerge. These natural leaders may be permanent or temporary leaders. They, too, will learn by doing. It should be abundantly clear that a prime consideration for the administrator is to encourage the kind of atmosphere in which the leadership can emerge. Although not all team teachers may wish to lead, those who have leadership abilities can add to their professional competency as they experience the opportunities to acquire and to develop the necessary abilities.

Student Leadership And Responsibility

Teachers in elementary schools often say that the students are not ready for leadership; high school will provide the opportunities. Teachers in high school often say that the students are not ready for leadership; college will provide the opportunities. Professors in college often say that the students are not ready for leadership; graduate school will provide the opportunities. Yet those students who survive the dropout rate and become graduate students often lament the lack of leadership and self-responsibility opportunities available under the direction of the university. It seems that the student is never ready, according to many teachers, to be a self-directed learner.

If teachers become involved in team teaching, the fallacy of postponing student leadership roles until the inevitable next year becomes quite evident.

Many opportunities exist for student leadership and self responsibility on the elementary and on the high school levels. On both levels, for example, student leaders can be used to chair discussions. Even children on the primary grade levels can and do think, are inquisitive, and make judgments. They talk to each other about ideas which are significant to them. One facet of team planning is the determination of the areas of knowledge and, at least at the outset, the specific questions to be used during small group discussions. The student leaders selected or elected, can meet with the teachers to receive instructions, to receive copies of the questions, and to be alerted to the importance of discussion. Obviously, the more mature

the student level, the more variety possible in the structure of the small group learning activity. Equally important, but not equally obvious, is that the student leader in first grade is capable of serving the capacity described. The teacher whose class is divided into two or more discussion groups at the same time can test immediately the validity of this statement. The depth of discussion may be quite minimal with some students, whether in grade one or grade 12, but the teacher who cannot be in contact with two groups at the same time will have to depend in some way and in some degree upon the student leader. Since the initial structure and guidelines are developed by the team of teachers they will be aware of what was expected during the discussion. The strengths and weaknesses of the student leader and his group can be factors to analyze and evaluate during team planning sessions. Leads obtained from the students can be built into large group presentations for review or for clarification or for further development. Also, test items can be derived from the types of discussions held. Moreover, the team can group and re-group the students for discussion purposes according to ability, interest and rapport with certain student leaders.

The students who are leaders in discussion sessions enjoy a status advantage as well as an academic role. The teachers can rotate the leadership or develop a cadre of specialists as they see fit. Regardless of the team decision, as student leadership becomes more expert and more acceptable through the grades, the students can become increasingly more involved in directing their own learning. If, for example, the student leaders demonstrate that they can chair discussions among peers effectively, the teacher may wish to allow the group to introduce its own questions for discussion purposes. The assumption is that the teachers can control the major thrust of the discussion through the list of questions provided but the needs of the group can be encouraged through some of its own questions. The divergence in outcomes of the several discussion groups becomes greater when each group and its leader are encouraged to pursue questions not provided by the teachers. This divergence will force the teacher to depend upon the summaries of the leaders if coordination of large-group, small-group and individual study is to be possible.

Certainly, the teacher is expected to be the professional leader he was educated to become. This role is not demeaned through the use of student leaders; his role is altered and enhanced. He and his team members are challenged to answer the basic questions concerning the purposes of small-group instruction, ways to evaluate it, and means of guiding it subtly but effectively. The team will have to plan lectures and demonstrations where its dominance is essential to the teaching-learning situation and from which can flow worthwhile discussion activities. The team teacher must also be able to coordinate the types of discussion which flow from the individual study and/or the independent study pursuits of some students. If the latter is to be possible, student leadership and student self-direction must be acknowledged. The distinct advantage of the team approach over the con-

22 ventional approach in this regard is that the team teachers can put their heads together to develop the means to derive the greatest possible advantages from student participation. Student leaders should not be regarded as threats to the teachers. The students will have certain ideas and insights which the teachers do not have. If these views are encouraged rather than ignored, the professional teachers can work with students on a meaningful level in order to guide or challenge or influence or direct or modify or corroborate these views.

The degree of control in the use of student leaders is the prerogative of the team of teachers. If the primary grade children, for example, are not considered to be ready for discussion, student leaders can be used for remedial help or for routine tasks of instruction. Students who can be the teacher's helper in these and in other ways can provide the teacher with the time to work with students who require special, professional assistance. If on any grade level the discussion seems to ramble too much, the teacher can provide additional structure to tighten the reins. If some students, leaders or followers, need additional help or freedom to profit from the pattern of large-group, small-group, and individual study, the teacher can use the time gained through student leadership and through team efforts to work with these special cases. Although an individual teacher can do some of these activities in a conventional school setting, the team approach provides greater flexibility; more and varied grouping possibilities; in-service, peer group stimulation from colleagues; and, if a modular schedule is used, more unscheduled time to work with students.

Without question the earlier the opportunities are afforded for student leadership and self-direction, the longer the period to develop skill and competence under the influence of professional teachers. Student leadership exists in the first grade. Graduate school is many years away for these young learners.

Guidelines for Implementation

Invariably, in speaking to educators about team teaching the question of how to begin is raised. Two colleagues, Mr. Charles B. Park and Mr. Harold Wilcox, both of Central Michigan University, have recommended that a list of specific guidelines be developed for inclusion in this Paper. Although their recommendation has been accepted, there is some danger in describing guidelines, steps, and structure. The following guides may be nothing more than following the letter and not the spirit of the innovation. One can learn to be a team teacher, of course, but the real success in team teaching and in team learning occurs when students and teachers pursue an intellectual interest because they must, because they have an intellectual thirst that cannot be quenched or ignored. When team teachers *feel* what has been described, they will need few guidelines. Because a beginning is necessary, however, suggested steps are in order.

The following guides are offered to teachers and to administrators who are interested in beginning a team teaching effort. Although most of these guides are teacher-oriented, some are administrator-oriented in the hope that not only the argument of who should initiate the project will be dispelled, but also the necessary cooperation between administrator and staff will be emphasized.

1. Gain administrative support. Accentuate the positive in your discus- sions.
2. Start by looking for someone on the staff with whom you can work cooperatively and effectively. This someone may be a teacher of the same subject or grade level, or he may be someone on another level or subject area. This teacher should be interested in experimentation and change.
3. Begin with those subjects which have the best possibilities for "blending." What is best often depends upon one's viewpoint. American literature and American history might not be a better blend than math and art in some schools.
4. Discuss the possibilities of sharing ideas, plans, lessons, and testing procedures with this partner. These discussions will iron out obvious problem areas.
5. If no headway is made, look for someone else to work with and start again.
6. After preliminary discussions are held and cooperation seems to be not only possible, but also desired, discuss the undertaking with your administrator.
7. Work cooperatively with the administration to provide similar schedules for the team teaching members.
8. Take time to have an orientation program which will cover at least these topics:

    a. Statements of school philosophy as they affect curriculum and methodology.
    b. Meaning of team.
    c. Nature and techniques of large-group, small-group, and individual study.
    d. Importance of details for team efficiency.
    e. Opportunities for teacher creativity.
    f. Differentiation of lectures, assignments, tests, and marks according to pupil ability.
    g. Use of audiovisual aids in large-group, small-group, and individual study.
    h. Role of guidance department, librarian, and "special" teachers.

The above topics can be treated for orientation purposes in approximately one week. To provide an example of "learn-by-doing," the topics can be presented in a large-group setting with opportunities for small-group discussions following each presentation.

The large-group presentations can incorporate those desirable features of lecture-demonstration techniques which are to be the model for the staff.

The small-group discussions can serve as object lessons in the importance of preparation prior to discussions, roles of participants, group dynamics, and other considerations.

Each team of teachers should be given time daily during the orientation program for lesson planning, development of visual aids, research, group meetings, and individual conferences. This involvement can serve as an example of individual study.

    9. Plan a sample lesson showing which points are to be taught through large-group presentation, small-group discussions, and individual study pursuits.

  10. Hold frequent meetings to evaluate progress.

     a. Allow teachers to make mistakes without fear of retribution.

     b. Encourage creative and original contributions from teachers.

     c. Encourage teachers to be self-critical, tempered by professional ethics.

     d. Make a sincere effort to accept the sound advice offered for the sake of improvement.

     e. Don't evaluate elusive outcomes too soon.

     f. Consider a variety of aspects to evaluate:

       1) Achievement of pupils.

       2) Amount and depth of subject matter covered.

       3) Opportunities for enrichment and correlation of subjects.

       4) Use of audiovisual aids.

       5) Use of library materials.

       6) Participation of pupils in discussion.

       7) Development of pupil self-responsibility.

       8) In-service advantages for teachers.

  11. Expand the team to include a third member whose academic strengths complement those of the other team members.

  12. Utilize the strengths of the team members. Do not merely "take turns."

  13. Criticize freely, openly, honestly, constructively, and professionally.

  14. Encourage administration to visit classes to criticize professionally and to improve the schedule.

  15. Invite the guidance personnel to participate in the development of lessons. Seek their suggestions concerning grouping of students, group dynamics techniques, and content emphases.

  16. Keep records of lessons, problem situations, and pitfalls for further evaluation and self-guidance.

  17. Keep communications clear and open.

  18. Take the necessary steps to refine and to improve the team approach.

In addition to the preceding remarks, administrators may be interested in the following guides which relate exclusively to their role in initiating a team teaching endeavor:

    1. Assess the climate for change.

    2. Try to determine who is ready to begin team teaching.

    3. Try to anticipate the reactions of the participants and of the rest of the staff.

    4. Try to assess the advantages and disadvantages involved.

    5. Determine the area most appropriate for the initiation of the change to team teaching.

    6. Inform the entire staff of the innovation even though only a few teachers will be involved.

    7. Allow interested staff members to participate.

8. Seek the cooperation of the entire staff.
9. Begin the team effort.
10. Be certain that the team teachers are adequately informed of purposes, guides, goals.
11. Give strong administrative support to the team teachers.
12. Provide time for planning the project *before* its inception *and* during its implementation.
13. Be sure that the schedules of the team teachers are similar or can be made similar. (This step minimizes scheduling problems at the outset.)
14. Expand the program through schedule provisions if success warrants this expansion.

Resource Centers

A resource center (sometimes called learning center or learning laboratory) is a designated place in the school where a specific subject or related subjects receive emphasis. Resource centers contain appropriate materials of instruction and have personnel assigned who have competence in the curricular areas emphasized. The centers may be located anywhere in the school building: in hallways, corners of classrooms, former offices, sections of the library, or—ideally—in special rooms equipped and staffed for the express purpose of the center. Furniture in classrooms can be rearranged, walls can be put up or taken down, and portable partitions can be used to create the physical space for such a resource center when the ideal is not possible. Wherever the location, the equipment should include at least tapes, charts, scale models, reference books, programmed materials, magazines, and slides. These materials can be used for drill purposes and directed study for those students who need this type of help. The materials and the professional staff may also be used as a stimulus to creative, independent study pursuits.

Analysis of these last two statements will make evident the need for professional decisions on the part of the team of teachers. Many students, in elementary schools and in high schools, do not have the interest, the motivation, nor the ability to be self-directed learners of academic offerings. These students need the structure and the direction provided by the professional staff. When these students, young or old, are in the resource center, the guidance and the supervision of a teacher will be necessary. This teacher, part of the team, will be aware of the content which was emphasized in large-group and in small-group sessions. Obviously, a flexible schedule and real team work are essential if the resource center is to be used most effectively for students who may not be able to work independently but who can work individually.

If there are several resource centers in a school and if teachers do not trust the judgment of the students to select that resource center which is most appropriate for their needs, students can be assigned to a specific center at specific times. Those students who appear to be able to budget their time, talent, and study interests effectively can be given free choice of study areas. These same students can also be permitted to engage in independent study pursuits. If and when abuses occur, the teachers can tighten the control factors which are theirs from the very outset.

Moreover, when several resource centers are established in a school, the selection of one instead of another may be an indication of a student's ability to be a self-directed learner. The serious student, even in grade one, is aware of some of his strengths and weaknesses. These students can study math in the math resource center where teachers of math are available for help if needed. A teacher of language arts or high school English can be of great aid to students who come to the language center to write poems, research papers, short stories, and compositions as well as to review grammar. Often two or three students have similar needs and interests which can be developed best in a resource center where individualization and independence can thrive.

At one time or another all of the teachers on the team will be assigned to a resource center. How students perform there will be a part of the professional responsibility of the team. The utilization of teacher talent and student ability requires close cooperation and the coordination of learning experiences that make a team a team.

Scheduling

The importance of a flexible schedule cannot be stressed too strongly. The team effort will fail unless the schedule provides the team teachers with opportunities to vary instructional approaches and to meet with each other and with students. Because the schedule can be so complicated, some administrators try to take short cuts by providing for only one phase of the program. This tactic is as shortsighted as it is unsound. All three phases are necessary for many reasons.

The large group, 80 to 100 to 200 or more students, is a teacher-dominated setting where visual aids are of inestimable value. While the teacher presents a lecture, a demonstration, or a question-and-answer session, he dominates, he controls, he structures the scope and the direction of the activity. The small group, twelve to eighteen students, is a student-centered activity where the teacher acts as a guide, a resource person. He is not a dominant figure in this learning situation. Discussion among peers is essential so that a free and open give-and-take concerning ideas and attitudes can exist. The individual study phase of the learning situation requires that one pupil and/or a small group of them pursue in depth some type of intellectual inquiry. Meaningful drill work is acceptable as a part of individual study, but the primary purpose goes beyond repetition and results in new and deeper insights, ideas, and approaches to thinking.

Some pupils will learn best in one of these settings, and others will learn best in another. Surveys of student attitudes about these phases reveal that they prefer the small-group discussion opportunities and that they like least individual study phases. The usual reason cited for the former is that the discussion provides an airing and a sharing of ideas with equals. The dislike for individual study is usually ascribed to a lack of knowledge of how to spend the time efficiently. Certainly, provocative assignments which are teacher initiated at first and student selected later can add to the value of independent study work as perceived by students.

Regardless of student preferences, all subjects have aspects which can be best taught to the total group, other aspects which require small-group

discussion, and still other aspects which require individual study pursuits.
The determination of these aspects is a fascinating task for teachers. When their decisions are successful, the learning of students and teachers can exceed the usual expectations.

Some teachers fail to realize that large-group instruction, small-group discussion, and individual study are interrelated. They are but three parts of the whole, and they must be recognized as such. Once recognized, the next step is to realize that it is easier to organize and to control the large-group presentation than to control the other two phases. When the teachers and the students begin a team teaching project, it is wise to provide much structure for the large-group activities. The structure can flow from the large group to the small group to the individual study with less and less structuring at each succeeding step. The process of going from the general to the particular is not new to teachers. When the teachers and the students gain more confidence and ability in small-group discussions and in independent study pursuits, the latter two phases will affect the nature and scope of the ensuing large-group presentations. The learning cycle will then proceed not only from the general to the particular but also from the particular to the general—from deduction to induction to deduction. The result will be an integrated, correlated, teaching-learning situation.

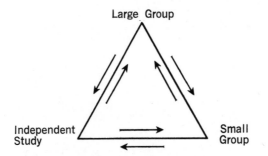

How, then, can the schedule enable team teaching to achieve its goals? Much flexibility can be derived by using simple block scheduling for those subjects and teachers to be involved in the team effort. For example, American history and American literature can be scheduled for two consecutive periods, from 9:00 to 9:50 and from 9:55 to 10:45. The block can be called American studies. The students can be called together in large-group sessions for lectures, they can be sub-divided into small groups for discussions, and/or they can be set free to study individually. The use of the time block can vary from day to day.

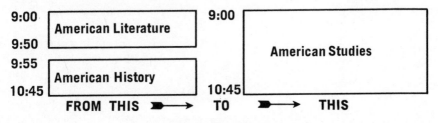

Many modifications on this model are possible, and each school can 29
expand the team teaching project to include more and more flexibility as
needed.

If more than two teachers are teamed, the flexibility can be increased
within the block as well as in other forms of scheduling. With the use of
large-group instruction the team of teachers can gain much time during the
school day for professional pursuits. Prior to a large-group presentation, the
team will plan general and specific aspects to be covered. When three or
four classes are combined for the large-group presentation (lecture, film,
filmstrip, demonstration, and so forth), it will seldom be necessary for the
entire team of teachers to be present. While one presents what the team has
planned and one teacher remains for evaluation and management assistance,
the other one or two teachers can be freed to work with accelerated or
remedial pupils, to do further planning, and to attend to other professional
duties, including assistance in the learning centers.

Even with a team of two teachers the time gained through the use of
large-group instruction is significant. The following chart, which uses English
as an example only, illustrates this point:

PERIOD	MONDAY		TUESDAY
	TEACHER A	TEACHER B	Teacher A and Teacher B
1	ENGLISH 10	ENGLISH 10	Large-Group Instruction (All Students in English 10)
2	ENGLISH 10	ENGLISH 10	↟
3	"FREE"	"FREE"	Planning Time
4	ENGLISH 10	ENGLISH 10	Pupil Conferences
5	LUNCH	LUNCH	Individual-Study Assistance
6	ENGLISH 10	ENGLISH 10	
7	ENGLISH 10	ENGLISH 10	↓

N.B. If the number of classes in a given subject or broad fields area does not approxi-
mate the number used in the chart, the application can be made to any situation by
using the first three or four periods indicated or the last three or four. Unfortunately,
experience with this illustration has shown that some administrators of small schools
see *only* that too many English classes are indicated to meet their needs.

Since all the students involved will have had their English 10 class by
the end of the first period on Tuesday, the teachers will be freed to perform
the professional tasks indicated. If individual study areas are not available
or if for some other reason the students have no place to go, the teacher
can provide supervised study time during the period when the students
regularly have English. This use of time is not recommended as a goal, but
it may be of some temporary value until the individual study time and
facilities can be utilized.

30   On days when large-group instruction is not scheduled, the teacher meets with the class in the "regular" room. Ideally, rooms designed for small-group discussions are to be used, but in the event they are not available, discussions can be held in the "regular" classroom. The teacher in each instance can divide the group into two or more sets. Guide questions can be provided, and student leaders can be used.

All the details concerning the factors which must be considered to effect such scheduling are beyond the scope of this treatment. For those who are interested in major schedule revisions which can provide a great degree of flexibility, the literature on modular scheduling may be of value. In this Paper the emphasis is on scheduled changes which a conventionally organized school can implement readily. In general, the main priority is to see that the large-group time is blocked out for all students and teachers who are involved in the team effort and that this time does not conflict with some other course which meets five days per week. Thus, although the example indicates that the large group be scheduled during the first period, it might be better placed during some other time in order to blend with art, music, physical education, shop, home economics, or some other subject which does not meet daily.

These "non-daily" subjects may include some of the major courses. There is much flexibility to be gained if subjects are scheduled fewer than five times per week. Keeping the total number of minutes per week constant, four fifty-minute meetings may unlock many schedule barriers which are posed by five forty-minute periods. The total number of minutes can be divided by five, four, or three without losing a minute of the total time. When classes do not meet daily, many typical scheduling problems disappear. Large-group and small-group sessions can be scheduled easily, and teachers can gain more time to plan and to work with individuals and with groups of two or three. Another possibility provided by the freer schedule is that enrichment subjects in the humanities, for example, can be built into the school day without overcrowding the usual course offerings.

On the elementary school level the question of scheduling for team teaching need not be difficult. If there are several sections of a given grade in the school, the combination possibilities for large group, small group and for individualized study activities are quite varied. If there is but one section of a given grade, acceptance of the non-graded concept for one or more subjects can provide the same type of variety in the organization of learning experiences. If the elementary school is departmentalized, the teachers in the same or in related departments can meet regularly to plan their work as stated in the preceding section on the secondary school.

Several questions concerning the scheduling of team teaching in elementary schools are raised frequently:

1. How can the teachers be given planning time?
2. How can young children learn in a lengthy large-group session?
3. How can "special" teachers be scheduled into the large-group, small-group, individual study pattern?
4. How can young children adjust to the varied schedule of classes, teachers, and class size?

A restructuring of some of the conventionally scheduled classes plus a
little imagination can resolve such questions. A modular schedule with long
and short periods provides a wide variety of options, but even minor
schedule revisions can be practical solutions. Administrative leadership and
the cooperation of the teachers involved will overcome whatever barriers
exist relative to schedule modification.

Team teachers must have time to plan and to prepare learning experiences if the team effort is to thrive. It is not a sound administrative approach
to expect that this planning be done outside of the school day even if the
teachers are willing to do this work on their own time. There must be time
for the organization of team efforts during the school day when fatigue,
other demands, and recreation do not interfere with the professionalism of
the teachers. Some of this necessary time can be gained if the teachers
utilize large group instruction. Teachers are accustomed to bringing several
classes together for movies, slides, filmstrips, assembly programs, and guest
speakers. These same classes can be brought together for lectures and
demonstrations which present new information, general concepts, reviews,
significant highlights, and for the purpose of testing. Perhaps the initial
planning for this first joint venture will have to be done after school. At
this planning session, all teachers involved will share in the planning of the
lecture so that all have information about the lesson, but the one with most
talent and interest will have the major responsibility for the instruction. A
second teacher probably should be present during the large group session
for professional evaluation and for management and control purposes. The
one or two other teachers on the team will thus be freed on school time to
plan for follow-up activities, to plan future demonstrations, and to confer
with other staff personnel.

An illustration may suffice. If three teachers on the fifth grade level, for
example, decide to team teach, they can determine at a planning session
what will be treated in a large group session in the subjects listed in the
charts below. The team can also decide who will be in charge of each
presentation and how to follow up the large group activity. On Monday,
then, the following can be put into effect:

	Teacher A	Teacher B	Teacher C
8:00-8:45	Math ————————————————————→		
8:45-9:30	←——————— Social Studies ——————→		
9:30-10:15	←———————————————————— Language Arts		

Teacher A will present the large group instruction to all three groups in
Math. Teacher B will present the Social Studies, and Teacher C will present
Language Arts. One of the teachers can be freed for other professional
pursuits while the two others are involved in the large group. As stated, all
three have participated in the planning session, and so no one is out of
touch with the instructional emphases.

32 On Tuesday, the three teachers can be in charge of their "regular" classes in the "regular" classrooms. The classes can be subdivided for small group discussion in "regular" classrooms if special discussion rooms are not available. The schedule on Tuesday, then, would look like this:

Tuesday

	Teacher A	Teacher B	Teacher C
8:00-8:45	Math	Math	Math
8:45-9:30	Social Studies	Social Studies	Social Studies
9:30-10:15	Language Arts	Language Arts	Language Arts

The time gained by freeing several teachers from the large group situation can be used to plan and to prepare individual study activities for students. If these activities and materials for individual study are not made available, the time gained for the teachers can be used up by individual conferences and special help which, however valuable, do not add to the opportunity for professional planning on school time. The teachers can purchase or develop tapes, charts, filmstrips, slides, work sheets, programmed materials, and manipulative devices which the students can use during their individual study time. Drill and practice items, self-tests, spelling words, names and places, dates and events, grammar exercises, and facts of all types for all subjects can be the content to be pursued if routine information is sought. Imaginative projects can be developed for those students who can go beyond the routine requirements. Whether such materials are purchased or constructed by the teachers, they need time to make decisions concerning the use and the evaluation of these items. Some of the necessary time will come from the large group activities as indicated and more time will come when the materials cited are used individually by the students according to their strengths and weaknesses. While the students, or a majority of them, are involved in these individualized pursuits, the teachers can allocate their supervising duties and rearrange classroom space so that several of those on the team are free to plan, prepare, and evaluate the learning activities. So that the entire team is kept aware of specific and general plans and procedures, clear communications are essential. When teacher talents are used effectively and communications are open, the isolation of a single teacher from the team efforts becomes a remote danger. Once aware of this possibility, however, the danger should never become real.

Similarly, many elementary school teachers and administrators fear that a long large group session is more than the attention span of young children can endure. No one knows for certain how much time a child or a group of them can attend a lecture and derive educational advantage from the experience. Rather than cite the potential dangers of lectures that are too long, the team teachers can insist that large-group sessions be short. How "long" and how "short" is a matter for professional judgment. Experience and experimentation will provide the answers.

In addition to the teachers who comprise the team there are opportunities for other teachers to become involved on occasion. There are schools which have the services of "special" teachers of art, music, speech, and physical education. If these teachers and the team teachers cooperate and communicate with each other so that instructional objectives are clear, some of the members of the team can be freed for other professional tasks, including planning time, while certain instructional activities are in progress. The physical education teacher can, if he is shown why, teach calisthenics to two or more classes at the same time. The music teacher can teach and play many songs to large groups of students at once. The art teacher can demonstrate many lessons to several classes simultaneously. Not only the classroom teachers gain from the freed time made possible by combining classes. The special teachers also gain time for conferring, planning, coordinating, and evaluating when two or three classes are brought together. Rather than restrict a schedule, the availability of special teachers can free a schedule so that valuable planning time for all becomes possible.

If special teachers are not available and the classroom teacher is required to teach music, art, and physical education, two or three teachers can use the team approach to gain time during the school day. These teachers can schedule art, for example, for their combined classes so that one teacher can take charge and the others can work on team activities. There are many activities in the elementary school which do not depend for success on low pupil-teacher ratios. Among these activities are group recitations, choral singing, listening to records, viewing art appreciation slides and films, relay games, and construction paper projects. One teacher can supervise most of these activities. If, however, one argues that two teachers are necessary, there is still the chance to free the third or fourth member of the team.

The teaching team can gain freed time in still another way. Three classes can be combined for reading or research, for example. Some of the children can be sent to the library, some can go to study areas in the classroom nooks or in study carrels set up in halls, offices, or in study centers. Care in pupil accountability is no problem if the teachers are cooperative and conscientious. Teacher aides can be used in this plan and in many other ways, including free and supervised reading time. By trusting students, by planning their activities, by involving other staff members and teacher aides, the team of teachers can gain enough planning time through minor schedule revisions to produce professionally rewarding results for themselves and for their students. Major schedule revisions can be an important next step.

It is essential for the team teachers to be aware that large-group, small-group and individual study activities are interrelated. Once recognized, the teachers can decide how often, for whom, and for what purpose each of these aspects will be utilized. With emphasis on the interrelationships of these aspects, there should be no problem of adjustment to various groups and to various teachers by the students, even those in the primary grades. The teachers who work as a team will be teaching *their* class, sometimes as a large group, sometimes as a small group, sometimes as individuals. The students will soon learn that the team is their teacher. Each child still has the option of identifying with his favorite teacher, but all the teachers are *his*.

Many schools have "special" personnel who are not usually considered an integral part of the educational program. Team teaching can help to overcome this viewpoint by including these staff members as part of the team. With a shift in emphasis the ensuing comments can be applied to all "special" teachers.

Although not all secondary schools have a guidance department, those which do offer the service can extend it very meaningfully in a team teaching setting. The opportunities for guidance personnel to help teachers to plan curricular offerings are enhanced in a team setting where regular and purposeful cooperation is expected and accepted. Theoretically, the guidance staff knows more than the classroom teacher about such psychological concerns as attention spans of children, effects of reward and punishment, pacing, evaluation of learning experiences, side effects of learning, and the like. During team planning sessions the guidance members can teach the teachers, directly and indirectly, about these psychological aspects, which are so integral a part of the teaching-learning situation.

For present or for future reference, the following suggested specific roles for the guidance department in team teaching are offered:

1. Plan with teachers on curriculum matters.
2. Participate in teaching activities of the team.
3. Teach teachers about the group dynamics of seminar activities.
4. Interpret test results for maximum efficiency in individual study pursuits of students.
5. Explain and demonstrate to staff members various means of evaluation.
6. Serve as a clearinghouse for staff members relative to major ideas in tests and measurements.
7. Help teachers with test construction.
8. Serve as sounding board and/or counselor for the staff.
9. Help teachers to realize the values of self-directiveness and individualization of instruction.
10. Teach teachers to have the guidance point of view.
11. Help the staff to understand some of the psychological considerations involved in *change*.

The following comments are offered as further elaborations on the topics relating to evaluation of students.

With the variety of means of evaluation available, one wonders why there is so much reliance upon paper-and-pencil tests. Whether it is the guidance personnel who inform teachers of other means of evaluation or whether the teachers help the guidance staff learn what evaluation means, it is expected that all involved in the team approach will learn a great deal from each other about the broad scope of evaluation. In spite of repeated admonitions found in the literature, many teachers—and perhaps guidance counselors—rely too heavily upon the traditional types of tests to assess pupil behavior.

A cursory survey of classroom procedures reveals the truth of this contention. There is no guarantee, of course, that a team effort will prevent overemphasis on such tests, but the involvement of many teachers should

make manifest the necessity to expand the concept of evaluation to include
such factors as:
1. Types of books read.
2. Types of questions and comments of students during small-group discussions.
3. Note-taking skills.
4. Use of time in individual study.
5. Types of individual study activities.
6. Indications of individual study pursuits brought into discussion.

Each of these means of assessing student performance has value, and the best utilization of each approach for each student is a topic worthy of team analysis. The talent and the knowledge of the guidance members of the team can prove to be of great benefit. If, as the case may be, the entire team is unfamiliar with intelligent alternatives to evaluation other than paper-and-pencil tests, a division of labor for research on the topic probably will provide the guidance personnel with an opportunity to show leadership. The results of the research can be discussed with advantage at team meetings.

The use of conventional testing will also provide an avenue for teamwork between classroom teachers and the guidance department. Complete texts on test construction are available, but not all teachers are familiar with the contents of these texts. Regardless of the reason for the lack of knowledge, the topic of test construction is often a well-known one to guidance personnel. Team teaching provides the continual opportunity for teachers to learn more about tests from their colleagues. Team teaching meetings can focus on such topics as essay and objective tests, avoiding pitfalls in wording (ambiguity, specific determiners, verbose statements, confusing directions, emphasis on obscure details), and the relationship of tests to the objectives set for the learners.

It is no secret that many teachers would welcome such help. Test construction requires knowledge and awareness that are not part of the repertoire of many teachers. The help rendered by the guidance staff can save a teacher many hours of painstaking labor. Just knowing that some of the knowledge sought in long essay items can be sampled by carefully chosen objective items, can be a boon to the harassed teacher.

If the guidance staff does not have some of the answers required by the teachers, the task is clear. With team effort, all involved gain in knowledge and, it is hoped, in competence.

Group Dynamics

Authorities in the field of group dynamics have much to offer the teacher who provides small group discussion opportunities for his students. These experts insist, for example, that there is leadership in every group. If the teacher can identify and utilize student leadership, the professional challenge of teaching is met with some success. It is not necessary for teachers to be expert in group dynamics, but the entire team must be aware of the importance of the factors which influence learning in a group situation. If they are willing to experiment with group composition, stimulus, and organization, much can be learned by doing. Team teachers can be of mutual help as they share insights about such concerns as the following relative to small-group discussions.

    a. Necessity of preparation and previous knowledge.

    b. Degree of structure—direction, types of questions, freedom, summary.

    c. Importance of "warm-up" period.

    d. Means of involving all members of the group.

    e. Means of utilizing titular and emergent leaders.

    f. Importance of physical setting.

    g. Means of evaluating participation and outcomes.

Teachers should make a concerted effort to provide students on all levels with many opportunities to have discussions. Even slow learners and immature learners can discuss ideas. The teachers can be of great assistance if they provide adequate structure for the groups according to their level of competence, interest, and experience.

At team meetings the teachers can develop guidelines for effective discussions which can be given to the students. These guidelines should emphasize the purposes of discussions as a learning situation and the importance of the contribution of each student to the total effort. These guidelines should be simple and should include such statements as these:

1. Respect each member of the group
2. Express your ideas clearly
3. Respect facts
4. Do not monopolize the discussion

The leader can be given guidelines of this type:

1. Involve as many participants as possible
2. Keep the discussion on a meaningful track
3. Tie loose ends together
4. Provide a summary of the discussion

More detailed and sophisticated statements can be presented after some familiarity with the basic approach has been developed. If the guidelines are too specific and too demanding at the outset, the results may be reluctance, hesitancy, confusion, and fear on the part of the students.

Another structural aid for the small group is the development of provocative discussion questions. Freewheeling, rambling, tangential discussions may lead to insights and new knowledge for some but the degree of freedom should be directly related to the "discussion competence" of the participants. Hence, the teacher can help the students begin their discussions by providing several open-ended, stimulating questions. These questions should seek implications and speculative responses based upon facts but not with facts as the end product. The year that Henry VIII ascended the throne of England is not very discussable. The results and implications of Henry's break with the Roman Catholic Church can be a fascinating and important discussion. When the students develop the awareness that "why?" questions are so valuable in the discussion phase of learning, they themselves can formulate interesting, provocative questions to supplement those which the teachers supply.

The types of questions asked and answered by students can be one means of evaluation by teachers. Teachers are often adept in determining the level of difficulty and sophistication of a question and an answer. They can apply this adeptness to the small-group discussion. They can be alert to which students are vocal and which are not. They can watch for the "silent language" of frowns, smiles, nods, and shrugs. The whole issue of differentiation among students and the dynamics of small-group instruction can be treated at team meetings.

With practice teachers and students can develop a high degree of proficiency in discussions. The students who are fortunate enough to engage in discussions on the elementary grade level will enjoy a distinct advantage over those whose practice and experience begin on the secondary school level. The team approach enhances the flexibility of grouping, discussing, and evaluating student performance. Knowledge of group dynamics can be developed and shared so that all involved can profit from the teaching-learning situation.

Visual Aids

Visual aids are of special importance in team teaching. Often the use of appropriate visuals makes the difference between an effective and an ineffective large-group presentation. In small-group sessions visual aids can evoke and stimulate discussion. Visuals can also be analyzed and interpreted as individual study activities. Testing can be done by presenting a visual which represents information and major concepts to which a student can be expected to react, interpret, evaluate. The very fact that a teacher develops a visual on a certain topic or aspect of the course is an indication of what he deems important and significant. With these and other factors to consider concerning the use of visual aids, it can be seen that professional judgments are necessary in this matter. The concerted, cooperative involvement of the team of teachers should result in an effective use of these aids.

Probably the most innovative and variable teaching aids in recent years are the overhead projector and the visual transparencies which they project. These aids have altered the physical, the psychological, and the instructional setting in hundreds of elementary and high schools throughout the land. Teachers can use visual aids and maintain a face to face relationship with their students. Teachers can demonstrate on the overhead projector color changes in chemical solutions due to reagents. Teachers can write in "natural sized" letters and 200-300 students in a large room will be able to read what has been written. The uses are so varied that the unimaginative teacher as well as the creative teacher can work comfortably with the projector.

The team approach to teaching can provide the necessary peer group pressures which teachers often need to demonstrate their originality in the use of these aids. Many commercially prepared visuals, especially transparencies, are available but these do not always meet the needs of a particular group of learners nor a particular topic which a team emphasizes. Even if this were not true, professional judgments would be necessary in order to select the most appropriate visual from the many offered by commercial concerns. Perhaps the consensus of the members of the teaching team is sufficient reason to select or reject certain visuals and this exercise of team effort is quite valuable.

More valuable, however, is the exercise of individual teacher creativity in the construction of ideas for visuals which the team must evaluate. The professional discussions attendant to the selection of ideas, the pictorial representation of them, and the determination of where and how to use them can be a great challenge to any team. This challenge is a curriculum matter, not a technical matter. Once determined by the team, a trained aide can make the visual aid. The professional role for the team is the creation of something for the aide to produce as a transparency. It is not easy to translate an abstract concept into a concrete, pictorial representation. The team of teachers will find much to ponder if they accept the professional challenge to develop significant visual aids for their students.

Pitfalls

The list of pitfalls which follows contains some of the difficulties encountered in team teaching. Not one of these pitfalls is a permanent obstacle, nor are many of them unique to team teaching. They loom as pitfalls in this context, however, because the necessary cooperation of teachers who work as a team brings these problems into a sharper focus than is customary in a conventional school.

Large-Group Instruction
1. Vocabulary too advanced for group.
2. Subject matter too complex or deep for group.
3. Insufficient differentiation among groups of pupils.
4. Failure to keep pace with pupil achievement.
5. Structure inappropriately organized for note-taking.
6. Topic difficult to discuss in seminar (small group).
7. Inadequate involvement of pupils.
8. Ineffective visuals.
9. Lack of team involvement in planning.
10. Failure to coordinate large-group presentations with small-group and individual study activities.

Small-Group Instruction
1. Too teacher-centered.
2. Ineffective use of pupil chairmen.
3. Use of seminar for non-seminar activities (reading, drill, and the like).
4. Superficial, "hot air" discussions by pupils.
5. Monopolization of discussion by a few.
6. Failure to summarize at end of class period.
7. Tangential discussions.
8. Poor control of impulsive participants.
9. Failure to coordinate small-group discussions with large-group and individual study activities.

Individual Study
1. Failure to provide enough material for pupils to work on individually.
2. Failure to motivate pupils sufficiently to do extra and/or deeper work.
3. Failure to circulate through study areas to give aid.
4. Insufficient resource materials.
5. Conflict between library and resource centers.

6. Inadequate pupil accountability.
7. Failure of pupils and teachers to understand purposes of individual study.
8. Failure to coordinate individual study activities with large-group and small-group activities.

Administration
1. Failure to communicate effectively with all concerned.
2. Difficulties with "touchy" teachers.
3. Failure to provide adequate in-service program, including orientation.
4. Inflexible schedule.
5. Failure to criticize effectively (pro and con).
6. Faulty selection of titular leaders.

Teachers
1. Formation of cliques with vested interests.
2. Failure to understand the meaning of a team.
3. Failure to plan far enough ahead.
4. Interest in gossiping.
5. Failure to pay attention to details.
6. Failure to develop appropriate evaluative techniques with team.
7. Failure to communicate with team members.

Opinionnaires

The following opinionnaire instruments (developed by M. P. Heller and E. Belford) may help administrators, teachers, and students to focus on some of the main aspects of team teaching:

Teacher Opinionnaire

Place a check mark in the appropriate column. Make your evaluations in terms of past experiences as a teacher or as a student teacher.

	Superior	Above Average	Average	Below Average	Poor
1. I rate the large-group lectures concerning:					
a. information contained					
b. interesting presentation					
c. ease of control					
2. I rate the seminars concerning:					
a. ease of control					
b. development of pupil leadership					
c. development of pupil responsibility					
d. utilization of factual knowledge by pupils					
3. I rate the individual study opportunities concerning:					
a. amount of time provided					
b. variety of types					
4. I rate the administration's interest in me					
5. I rate the opportunities in in-service education concerning:					
a. suggestions for improvements in methodology					

	Superior	Above Average	Average	Below Average	Poor
b. availability of resources pertinent to my teaching field					
c. involvement in curriculum planning					
d. opportunities to continue formal education					
e. opportunities to develop professional strengths					
6. I rate the opportunities for teacher creativity concerning:					
a. free hand in conducting classes					
b. opportunity to experiment with varied approaches to classroom management					
c. opportunities to develop differentiated pupil assignments					
7. I rate the opportunities for teacher leadership concerning:					
a. opportunities to develop professional strengths					
b. opportunities to influence team members					
8. I rate the leadership of team chairmen concerning:					
a. development of an atmosphere in which I can work well					
b. provision of opportunities for me to engage in planning					
c. implementation of the basic objectives of our program					
d. willingness to work long hours on school problems					
e. availability for personal conferences					
f. formulation of directions so that I know what is expected of me					
9. I rate the leadership of the administration concerning:					
a. development of an atmosphere in which I can work well					
b. provision of opportunities for me to engage in planning					
c. implementation of the basic objectives of our program					
d. management of details					
e. willingness to work long hours on school problems					
f. availability for personal conferences					
g. formulation of directions so that I know what is expected of me					
10. I rate the effectiveness of the team teaching approach concerning:					
a. cooperative planning					
b. opportunities to learn from team members					
c. opportunities to influence team members					
11. I rate the total program					

12. What do you like best about the team teaching program?
13. What do you like least about the team teaching program?
14. Do you prefer a conventional program to this program?

Pupil Opinionnaire

Place a check mark in the appropriate column. Make your ratings by comparing each statement below with your school situation last year.

	Superior	Above Average	Average	Below Average	Poor
1. I rate the large-group lectures concerning:					
a. information contained					
b. interesting presentation					
c. feeling of my own participation .					
2. I rate the seminars concerning:					
a. helping overcome shyness					
b. giving opportunity to express opinions					
c. making ideas clearer by discussions					
d. increasing feeling of responsibility for learning					
e. stimulating my interest in related ideas					
f. encouraging the beginning of individual research or projects					
3. I rate individual study opportunities concerning:					
a. variety of types					
b. availability of study materials					
c. availability of teachers to help....					
d. freedom to use time on projects or individual research					
4. I rate the teachers' interest in me ...					
5. I rate the opportunities to learn					
a. in large group					
b. in seminar					
c. with teacher help					
d. on my own					
6. I rate opportunities for pupil leadership					
a. in seminar					
b. in individual study					
c. in extracurricular activities					
7. I rate the development of self responsibilities					
a. in seminar					
b. in individual study					
c. in extracurricular activities					
8. I rate the number of facts learned					
a. in lecture					
b. in seminar					
c. in individual study					
d. in comparison with other schools					
9. I rate the opportunities for being original					
10. I rate the total program					

42 *Supervisory Checklist*

The checklist presented here suggests certain factors for the evaluation of team teachers. This list may be used for an official visit, and it may be used by the team members themselves for peer supervision as well as for self-analysis. Some of the factors included are of the type which are usually found in supervisory checklists. Familiarity. with such factors may provide team teachers with a sense of comfort so that the "new" items will not be unduly threatening. It is essential, of course, that "new" or "old" the factors be evaluated in a team teaching context.

Teacher observed _____ Date _____

Activity observed (encircle one) : large group, small group, lab, individual study

Time spent in observation _____

Follow-up conference with teacher   Yes _____   No _____

Use a check (√) to evaluate the teacher performance for each appropriate listing:

	Superior	Above Average	Average	Below Average	Poor
1. Pupil attention					
2. Pupil participation					
3. Use of visuals					
4. Use of student chairman					
5. Pace of lecture					
6. Appropriateness of vocabulary					
7. Use of summary techniques					
8. Preparation of teacher					
9. Rapport between teacher and class					
10. Guidance of small-group discussion					
11. Organization of topic for note-taking purposes					
12. Type of assignment given					
13. Assistance given during I. S.					
14. Evidences of team planning					
Other comments:					

Supervisor: _____

WHY TEAM TEACHING?

Change is here. Current dissatisfaction with education on all levels gives impetus to the clamor for more change. Innovations which are embraced without a thought about the why and wherefore concerning them merely add to the resulting confusion. The Hawthorne effect may produce sufficient psychological advantages for those involved in change to warrant change for its own sake, but for those who resist such a reason, the innovation of team teaching can stand on its own merits. Although team teaching as a total approach is yet to be evaluated definitively, there is little in team teaching that has not been researched and evaluated in some way in connection with and apart from the team teaching per se. For example, the lecture techniques have been tools of effective teaching for centuries. For another example, work with group dynamics leaves little doubt that students can learn much from each other. Discussions among peers have been evaluated in many studies as productive learning experiences. Students who are motivated to study as independent learners have demonstrated repeatedly that 43 they can reach levels of great depths of knowledge. Team teaching incorporates all of these aspects into the total learning experience.

Team teaching requires the cooperative, purposeful efforts of two or more teachers whose academic and personal competencies complement each other. If these teachers can work together effectively, the learning experiences which they develop should be more meaningful for them and for their students than those experiences which are developed in the isolation of a mental vacuum. We do not live in a vacuum, we do not think in a vacuum; therefore, why should we teach in a vacuum? Why not reap the benefits of peer-group stimuli made possible by two, three, four, or more excellent, competent professionals who can work together for the purpose of improving teaching and learning for themselves and for their students Team teaching can be an answer to these questions.

EPISODES FOR ANALYSIS

The following episodes have been selected to highlight some of the situations which arise when teachers become involved in team teaching.

In each instance, the episode should raise questions and alternatives which challenge the professional insights of administrators and teachers alike. An analysis of each episode can be a valuable experience at faculty meetings, at administrative sessions, and at orientation meetings. The episodes are intended to provoke reactions which each reactor can attempt to justify. There is no single acceptable course of action implied. Some of the variables involved in these episodes apply to any teaching situation, but the team approach heightens their importance.

What is the key issue in each situation? What are important secondary issues? What alternatives can be developed? What would you do in each situation?

Miss Jones is a member of the fourth grade teaching team in Language Arts in a large elementary school. The principal is convinced that Miss Jones has leadership ability and she has encouraged Miss Jones to be involved in team teaching. Miss Jones has agreed readily. During planning sessions, Miss Jones often asks questions of the three other team members which relate to the advantages and the problems involved in teaching as a team. The fellow team members have been sincere in their attempts to answer Miss Jones's questions, but there are the beginnings of resentments and irritations because much valuable planning time has been taken up for Miss Jones's purposes, rather than for curricular concerns.

In addition to the time taken up during planning sessions as a result of the methodological and "philosophical" questions of Miss Jones, many fruitless sessions have transpired because Miss Jones seems to be unwilling to share ideas and to accept ideas of other team members. Miss Jones is seldom receptive to the ideas of the other team teachers, and she has shown reluctance to follow the plans, even though they have been agreed upon by all. This reluctant agreement has become a pattern for Miss Jones. The other team members have formed a clique which excludes Miss Jones, and Miss Jones is aware of this. Miss Jones has complained to the principal that the three members are not cooperative.

Mr. Heath is the appointed leader of the teachers who are team teaching in Biology in a large high school. There are four teachers on the team including Mr. Heath. Mr. Heath is very knowledgeable in the field of Biology. He has published three articles in the field and he has received two summer fellowships in Biology at two different universities. Two of the other team members have received a fellowship in Biology at a summer institute.

Mr. Heath holds planning sessions at least once per week with the team members. At these meetings, Mr. Grant is usually the one who makes the suggestions which the rest of the team accepts as learning experiences, including lab demonstrations. The other team members give no indication that they feel stifled in offering their suggestions, but Mr. Grant seems to be the leader of the group in planning sessions. Mr. Heath and Mr. Grant have maintained very cordial relationships. Mr. Heath is regarded by the team as the appointed leader and his assignments and professional obligations are accepted without negative responses. The influence of Mr. Grant was noticed by the principal who attended first one, then several other sessions of the Biology team.

Mr. Black and Miss White are very enthusiastic about team teaching. They have read a great deal about the topic and they have discussed ways of combining their courses, American Literature and American History, into an integrated whole. They have developed several lessons with large-group, small-group, and individual study phases. They are very compatible personally and professionally.

They have asked Mr. Chesley, the principal, for permission to begin teaming. Mr. Chesley is undecided about granting this permission. He is uncertain about several factors, including the reactions of other staff members, the means of revising the schedule to accommodate the team effort, and the implications of his role as administrator of a team project.

Mr. White, Miss Green, and Mrs. Blue, three teachers on the sixth grade level, have been asked by their principal to begin team teaching during the next school year. The teachers have agreed and they have started to plan. By general agreement the plan for the next year will be thus: Mr. White will teach mathematics and science, Miss Green will teach the language arts, and Mrs. Blue will teach social studies. The schedule will provide for the teaching of these subjects so that each sixth grader will go from Mr. White to Miss Green to Mrs. Blue for the solid subjects in the morning. During the afternoons each teacher will be responsible for art, music, health, penmanship, etc.

The three team teachers are satisfied that this arrangement will allow for specialization. The principal is pleased that his suggestion to begin team teaching has been well received. The principal is not satisfied with the arrangement of classes, but he is anxious for the team effort to begin.

Mr. Blue is a member of the eleventh grade teaching team in U. S. History. There are two other team members. The team teaching approach includes large-group lectures, small-group discussions with pupils, and individual study activities.

Each teacher of the team is required to participate in all three phases of instruction. Independent study has not yet been developed and so the students spend much time in drill work, homework assignments, and browsing through history books and periodicals. Mr. Blue has been observed by the principal on several occasions in the faculty lounge instead of being present in the assigned area for individual study. The principal has asked Mr. Blue whether he sees an advantage in individual study for students. Mr. Blue has said "yes" although he is not satisfied with the routine practices in which most of the students are engaged. He hopes to see each student engaged in research projects. When this hope has been realized, Mr. Blue has stated that he will be willing to guide these research projects for the interested students. In the meantime, however, the dissatisfaction with the routine aspects of the students' activities has made him disinterested in supervising their study time. The principal suggested that Mr. Blue work with some of the students to lead them from their present state to the one of independent intellectual inquiry. In order for this leadership to be possible, Mr. Blue's presence in the study area is important. Mr. Blue agreed.

In the weeks that followed, Mr. Blue continued to leave unattended the 18 to 20 students assigned to him for study purposes. The group of students has become increasingly noisy and rowdy, and several filmstrips have been destroyed.

Miss Green is a member of a team of three teachers of tenth grade math. She has four years of teaching experience including two years as a team teacher. Miss Green is very pleased with her work in small group instruction. She considers the large-group presentations to be too difficult for the students. She explains the major points of the large-group lectures and demonstrations to the small group and then she quizzes the students on the information covered. Miss Green is pleased when her students master the salient points of the topic. As a reward for the successful students, Miss Green excuses them from individual study assignments.

Miss Gemson is a member of a three woman team of teachers in language arts on the fifth grade level. She is an outspoken young lady who has had three years of teaching experience although this is her first year as a team teacher. The two other teachers are in their first year of teaching and they have shown some deference to Miss Gemson's experience.

After one month of the school year has gone by it has become evident to the supervisor, the principal and to the two teachers that Miss Gemson has taken the reins of the planning sessions. She organizes the lecture schedule, she selects the lecture topics, and she assigns duties to other teachers for individual study work. She has shown that she is reluctant to accept the suggestions of her two team members and some ill will is beginning to develop. What Miss Gemson says is generally academically sound, but the impending personality clash seems to be evident to all concerned except Miss Gemson.

The principal has decided to add a fourth teacher to the team, and he selected a willing, conscientious, extroverted young man who is in his second year of teaching although this year is his first year as a team teacher. After two weeks of the formation of the four-teacher team, Mr. Gray has told Miss Gemson that he finds it difficult to plan with her since she plans for everyone. Miss Gemson began to cry. She stormed out of the meeting room, and she went to the principal's office. She told the principal that Mr. Gray's presence on the team has ruined the cooperative spirit that had developed during the semester and that unless he apologizes and begins to cooperate she will not remain a part of the teaching team.

Mr. Benson is the principal of a large high school in which three teams are in operation. Each team began team teaching during the current school year after a four-week pre-school orientation program. Mr. Benson is pleased with the initial efforts of each team, but he wants to provide the teachers with an in-service education program. When Mr. Benson approached the teams with his plan, they balked at the idea. Each team indicated that the time necessary for in-service education would use up valuable planning time. The teachers also stated that they learned enough about team teaching during the summer program to be able to profit from "learn by doing" experiences.

An attempt to list the many articles on team teaching would merely duplicate the efforts of others who have compiled such lists. The following information, however, should serve those who are interested in pursuing the topic further:

Books:

Bair, Medill, and Woodward, Richard G. *Team Teaching in Action.* Boston: Houghton Mifflin Company, 1964. 229p.

Beggs, David W. (ed.). *Team Teaching: Bold New Venture.* Bloomington: Indiana University Press, 1965. 192p.

Shaplin, Judson T., and Olds, Henry F., Jr. (eds.). *Team Teaching.* New York: Harper and Row, 1964. 430p.

Trump, J. Lloyd, and Baynham, Dorsey. *Focus on Change—Guide to Better Schools.* Chicago: Rand McNally and Company, 1961. 147p.

N.B. Bibliographies are included in the above.

Pamphlets:

Heller, Melvin P. *Team Teaching.* Cleveland: Educational Research Council of Greater Cleveland, 1963. 45p.

Trump, J. Lloyd. *Images of the Future.* Washington: NASSP, 1959. 46p.

Bibliographies:

National Education Association, 1201 Sixteenth Street, N.W., Washington, D.C. 20036 6p.

Indiana University, School of Education, Bloomington, Indiana. 16p.

Center for Team Teaching, Weber County Schools, 1122 Washington Blvd., Ogden, Utah 84404.

NASSP *Bulletin:* January issues. 1958-1962.

Designed, produced, and distributed by Geo. A. Pflaum,
Publisher, Inc.

NCEA Papers: *No. 1 The Parish School Board, by Rev.
Olin J. Murdick*
*No. 2 Team Teaching: A Rationale, by
Melvin P. Heller, D.Ed.*

Subscriptions to NCEA Papers (five titles, bimonthly, September through May)
are obtainable at $7.50 per subscription. Copies of individual titles are available
at $1.50 per copy. Discounts on quantity orders of individual titles are: 10 percent
on 7-13 copies; 20 percent on 14 or more copies. On orders of less than $5.00 not
accompanied by payment, a 45-cent postage-handling charge will be added.

National Catholic Educational Association
NCEA Papers, Box 667, Dayton, Ohio 45401